The Majestic Fourteeners . . .

COLORADO'S HIGHEST

The Majestic Fourteeners...

COLORADO'S HIGHEST

PHOTOGRAPHED BY GEORGE CROUTER

Edited by Carl Skiff

A SUNDANCE PICTORIAL

SUNDANCE
Books

The Majestic Fourteeners...

COLORADO'S HIGHEST

PHOTOGRAPHED BY GEORGE CROUTER

Edited by Carl Skiff

Graphical presentation —
   Sundance Publications, Ltd., Silverton, Colorado

Photolithography —
   Publishers Press, Salt Lake City, Utah

Binding —
   Mountain States Bindery, Salt Lake City, Utah

Editor-in-Chief — Russ Collman
Production Manager — Dell A. McCoy
Color Separations — Steven J. Meyers

ISBN 0-913582-22-0

First Printing — July, 1977

FOREWORD

If we look for grandeur in mountain form, what is more grand than the great mountain under our feet?
                            Franklin Rhoda, Hayden Survey, 1875

A century later, George Crouter, veteran photographer for *The Denver Post*, swallowed hard as he recalled a trip into the high country of Colorado. "A chill ran up and down my spine," he said, "and I had to fight back the tears as I stood in the midst of those beautiful mountains and looked out over what seemed hundreds of peaks, all rising ever so majestically. I was so awe-stricken by my surroundings that it was several minutes before I could get about my business."

Crouter's business was photographing *Colorado's Highest* — all of the state's 53 peaks with elevations of 14,000 feet or more, commonly known as the Fourteeners.

Crouter traveled hundreds of miles — on foot and horse, in car, four-wheeler and plane — to put together what turned out to be one of the most popular series ever published by *Empire Magazine*, the Sunday magazine of *The Denver Post*. Most of the photographs in this book first appeared in the 28-part series that *Empire* ran during 1976 as a tribute to Colorado's Centennial as a state and the nation's Bicentennial birthday.

Six years before Colorado gained statehood, a then-obscure photographer in Omaha, Nebraska, 27-year-old William Henry Jackson, was hired by Ferdinand Vandeveer Hayden to work with him in his survey of the Western territories. Hayden, whose surveys (including four of Colorado, 1873 through 1876) laid the foundations for much of our knowledge of the Rocky Mountains, recognized the importance of photography in "securing truthfulness in the representation of mountains and other scenery."

In a March 15, 1877, letter to Secretary of the Interior Carl Schurz, Hayden emphasized the significance of photographs in "securing faithful views of the many unique and remarkable features of newly explored territory." Truth in pictures was particularly important because some art forms had been giving false notions to people back East of how our Western mountains really looked. "Twenty years ago," Hayden wrote, "hardly more than caricatures existed — mountains were represented with angles of 60 degrees inclination, covered with great glaciers, and modeled upon the type of any other than the Rocky Mountains."

And so Jackson and other journalists accompanied the Hayden geographical and geological surveys; their reports, writings and photographs greatly popularized the West. It was Jackson who first photographed the Mount of the Holy Cross in Colorado's Sawatch Range, and Hayden's men were the first to write about the ancient Indian cliff dwellings of Mesa Verde in southwestern Colorado. The Hayden men and their guests combined scientific skill, artistic sketching, photographic techniques and stamina as they worked the Colorado mountains from predawn to nightfall. The pleasures of their work came, as they did to photographer George Crouter, in the compensating scenic surroundings. The Hayden men, although preoccupied in their mapping, surveying, sketching and figuring, still found time to enjoy and marvel at the snow-capped peaks, as well as the fertile valleys below and the wildlife that have always called the mountains their home.

Colorado is the highest and most mountainous state in the contiguous United States, with an average elevation of nearly 7,000 feet. And, as one reader, David Sundal of Grand Junction, Colorado, wrote to *Empire Magazine*: "Mighty mountains are what we Coloradans find most inspiring about our state."

As long as there are mountains, there will, be men and women to enjoy them and photographers (like 19th Century Jackson and 20th Century Crouter) to photograph them. And, it is comforting to know that these mountains belong to you and me. Thus, it is to all of us who enjoy, respect, love and admire the mountains of Colorado that this book is dedicated.

Carl Skiff, Editor
Empire Magazine

CONTENTS

Page

Foreword 5
Altitudes of Colorado's Fourteeners 8
Acknowledgments 9

SECTION ONE

Map of Sangre de Cristo and Culebra Ranges   10
Sangre de Cristo and Culebra Ranges   11 thru 25

Photographs
1 Culebra Peak 12, 13
2 Mount Lindsey 14, 15
3 Blanca Peak 16, 17, 18, 19, 20, 21
4 Little Bear Peak 16, 17, 18, 19
5 Kit Carson Peak 22, 24
6 Crestone Peak 22, 23, 25
7 Crestone Needle 22, 23, 25
8 Humboldt Peak 23, 25

SECTION TWO

Map of the Front Range 26
Front Range .... 27 thru 47

Photographs
9   Pikes Peak 28, 30, 31
10 Mount Evans 33, 34, 35
11 Mount Bierstadt 36, 37
12 Grays Peak 38
13 Torreys Peak 40
14 Longs Peak 42, 43, 44, 47

SECTION THREE

Map of Mosquito and Tenmile Ranges 48
Mosquito and Tenmile Ranges ...... 49 thru 59

Photographs
15 Mount Sherman 50, 51
16 Mount Bross 52, 53
17 Mount Lincoln 54, 55
18 Mount Democrat 56, 57
19 Quandary Peak 58, 59

SECTION FOUR

Map of the Sawatch Range 60
Sawatch Range .... 61 thru 92

Photographs
20 Tabeguache Mountain 62, 63
21 Mount Shavano 62, 64, 65
22 Mount Antero 66, 67
23 Mount Princeton 68, 70, 71
24 Mount Yale 72
25 Mount Columbia 74, 75
26 Mount Harvard 76, 77
27 Mount Oxford 78, 79
28 Mount Belford 78
29 Missouri Mountain 78
30 Huron Peak 80
31 La Plata Peak 82, 83
32 Mount Elbert 84, 86
33 Mount Massive 86, 88, 89
34 Mount of the Holy Cross 90, 92

SECTION FIVE

Map of the Elk Range 94
Elk Range .... 95 thru 111

Photographs
35 Castle Peak 96, 97
36 Pyramid Peak 99, 100, 101
37 Maroon Peak 102, 103, 104, 106
38 North Maroon Peak 102, 103, 104, 106
39 Snowmass Peak 108, 109
40 Capitol Peak 110, 111

SECTION SIX

Map of San Juan and San Miguel Ranges   112
San Juan and San Miguel Ranges   .. 113 thru 143

Photographs
41 San Luis Peak 115
42 Handies Peak 116, 117
43 Redcloud Peak 119, 120
44 Sunshine Peak 120, 121
45 Uncompahgre Peak 122, 123
46 Wetterhorn Peak 122, 123, 124, 125
47 Mount Eolus 126, 127
48 Sunlight Peak 128, 129
49 Windom Peak 130, 131
50 Wilson Peak 132, 133, 136
51 Mount Wilson 133, 136
52 El Diente Peak 133, 134, 136
53 Mount Sneffels 138, 139, 141, 143

Map on opposite page drawn by Joe Barros.

How They Are Ranked . . .
Altitudes of Colorado's Fourteeners

Number	Mountain	Elevation
1.	Mount Elbert	14,433
2.	Mount Massive	14,421
3.	Mount Harvard	14,420
4.	La Plata Peak	14,336
5.	Blanca Peak	14,345
	Ellingwood Peak	14,042
	(Considered part of Blanca Peak)	
6.	Uncompahgre Peak	14,309
7.	Crestone Peak	14,294
8.	Mount Lincoln	14,286
	Mount Cameron	14,238
	(Considered part of Mount Lincoln)	
9.	Grays Peak	14,270
10.	Mount Antero	14,269
11.	Torreys Peak	14,267
12.	Castle Peak	14,265
	Mount Conundrum	14,022
	(Considered part of Castle Peak)	
13.	Quandary Peak	14,265
14.	Mount Evans	14,264
15.	Longs Peak	14,255
16.	Mount Wilson	14,246
17.	Shavano Peak	14,229
18.	Mount Princeton	14,197
19.	Mount Belford	14,197
20.	Crestone Needle	14,197
21.	Mount Yale	14,196
22.	Mount Bross	14,172
23.	Kit Carson Mountain	14,165
24.	El Diente Peak	14,159
25.	Maroon Peak	14,156
26.	Tabeguache Mountain	14,155
27.	Mount Oxford	14,153
28.	Mount Sneffels	14,150
29.	Mount Democrat	14,148
30.	Capitol Peak	14,130
31.	Pikes Peak	14,110
32.	Snowmass Mountain	14,092
33.	Windom Peak	14,087
34.	Mount Eolus	14,084
	North Eolus	14,039
	(Considered part of Mount Eolus)	
35.	Mount Columbia	14,073
36.	Missouri Mountain	14,067
37.	Humboldt Peak	14,064
38.	Mount Bierstadt	14,060
39.	Sunlight Peak	14,059
40.	Handies Peak	14,048
41.	Culebra Peak	14,047
42.	Mount Lindsey	14,042
43.	Little Bear Peak	14,037
44.	Mount Sherman	14,036
45.	Redcloud Peak	14,034
46.	Pyramid Peak	14,018
47.	Wilson Peak	14,017
48.	Wetterhorn Peak	14,015
49.	North Maroon Peak	14,014
50.	San Luis Peak	14,014
51.	Huron Peak	14,005
52.	Mount of the Holy Cross	14,005
53.	Sunshine Peak	14,001

U. S. Geological Survey

F. V. HAYDEN and the men of his survey were the first to climb many of Colorado's Fourteeners.

Acknowledgments

We are indebted to a number of people, places and things for helping make this book possible, including foremost *The Denver Post*, which first published George Crouter's photographs in its Sunday *Empire Magazine* during 1976.

Among those assisting in the project were the U.S. Forest Service, the Colorado Division of Wildlife, Ron Jackson of Lake City, Colorado (his four-wheeler got Crouter into some rough terrain), and Ray Hill of Lakewood, Colorado. Hill is chief of the National Cartographic Information Center (Rocky Mountain Mapping Center) located at the Denver Federal Center. A veteran climber himself, Hill brought out map upon map, plus many recollections of his own, to identify many of the Fourteeners for us.

Altitudes of the peaks featured in this book are based on the latest information compiled from U.S. Geological Survey maps or mapping operations, and the U.S. Coast and Geodetic Survey. In some cases, elevations will differ from those published elsewhere, but we are treating the altitudes listed herein as "official."

In compiling the text that accompanies Crouter's striking color photos, we turned to several sources, including *Great Surveys of the American West*, by Richard A. Bartlett; *Guide to the Colorado Mountains*, by Robert Ormes with the Colorado Mountain Club; *The Fourteeners*, by Perry Eberhart and Philip Schmuck; a number of stories and letters in *Empire Magazine*; and, most important, four volumes in the Denver Public Library's Western History Collection: The annual reports (1873 through 1876) of *The United States Geological and Geographical Survey of the Territories Embracing Colorado* that geologist Ferdinand Vandeveer Hayden and his men assembled.

We also appreciate the cooperation of the U.S. Geological Survey in making available photos showing men of the Hayden Survey exploring the mountains of Colorado. These photos we have used to complement the color photos by Crouter and to pay tribute to the great work accomplished by these surveys.

The maps in this book were drawn by Joe Barros of *Empire Magazine*.

As with all history, controversies and arguments abound in discussions of origins of mountains' names, the significance of certain peaks, their elevations and who climbed them first. In some instances, separating truth, fiction and legend was difficult.

If only the mountains could speak, we would be able to obtain the "real story."

Thus, we offer this book not as an answer to any controversy, but as a means to better enjoy the highest peaks in Colorado and to become a little better acquainted with their history.

Section One . . .

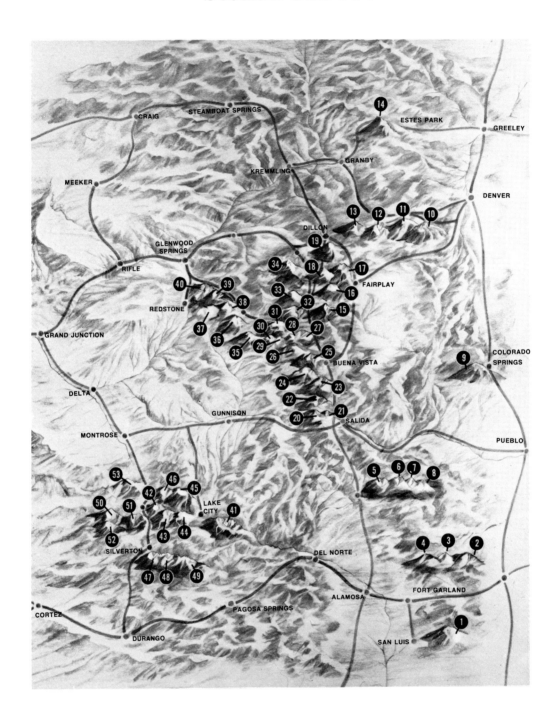

1	Culebra Peak	**5**	Kit Carson Peak
2	Mount Lindsey	**6**	Crestone Peak
3	Blanca Peak	**7**	Crestone Needle
4	Little Bear Peak	**8**	Humboldt Peak

Sangre de Cristo and Culebra Ranges

Ascending the highest mountain of the range, Blanca Peak, we have a view that richly repays the fatigue and danger of the climb.

F. M. Endlich, Hayden Survey, 1875

"He-who-picks-up-stones-while-running" was the name given by the Indians to the slightly built, bearded white man who climbed over and around Colorado's lofty mountains in the mid-1870s. The red men found Ferdinand Vandeveer Hayden and his party a curious lot, and maybe at times considered them intruders, but for the most part let these 19th-Century explorers go about their business. For Hayden, a medical doctor who became a renowned geologist, and his men were peaceful, hard-working, determined and even passionate in their "geological and geographical survey of the territories, embracing Colorado."

These were the men — geologists, artists, topographers, photographers, anthropologists, botanists, paleontologists, entomologists, agriculturalists — who scaled, for the first time in some instances, many of Colorado's Highest — the majestic Fourteeners rising to above-sea elevations of 14,000 feet or more. They collected rocks, studied flora and fauna, observed, classified and explored the mountains. They found the presence of bears annoying and comically frustrating; they flirted with death during highly charged electrical storms; they battled their way through snow, rain and dust storms; they encountered forest fires with perturbation (the smoke would obscure their sightings of the peaks and the fallen logs would slow their progress). And, the very mountains themselves presented problems — how would they be climbed, and where were the safest trails?

But, in the process of going about their daily chores of climbing, recording and mapping, the survey men became overwhelmed by the scenery, and these feelings, too, were recorded along with the bare statistics of mountains, rocks, flowers and insects.

For instance, atop Culebra Peak, the southernmost Fourteener in Colorado, Franklin Rhoda was fascinated by wind-and-cloud movement. Rhoda, a young topographer for Hayden who later became a Presbyterian minister, wrote in his 1875 report:

It was interesting to see how the clouds were gradually consumed before the wind from the north. The manner in which they melted away before the dry air...was curious in the extreme.

Culebra Peak, Colorado's 41st highest at 14,047 feet, is part of the Culebra Range that runs south 30 miles from La Veta Pass to the New Mexico boundary. Culebra in Spanish means "snake," a name first given to a creek on the peak's slopes. Culebra Peak is southeast of the oldest town in the state, San Luis, on Colorado Highway 159.

Up from the Culebra Range, north of U.S. Highway 160, is the Sangre de Cristo Range, a Spanish name for "Blood of Christ" — referring to the alpine glow of sunrise. On the map, as Robert Ormes explains in his *Guide to the Colorado*

Culebra Peak in southern Colorado, looking toward the southeast (above), with another view (opposite page) looking northeast.

CULEBRA

LINDSEY

Mountains, the Sangre de Cristo chain, which runs 75 miles south-southeast from Salida to Sierra Blanca, is an exclamation point — a long straight line of peaks with the Blanca group forming a detached dot below. The Sierra Blanca includes three official Fourteeners — Mount Lindsey, Blanca Peak and Little Bear Peak — and one unofficial — Ellingwood Peak.

Hayden and his men found the Sierra Blanca most impressive. In his 1876 report, he wrote:

> About six miles north of Fort Garland is one of the highest and most rugged mountain peaks in the West, called Blanca Peak, principal summit of the Sierra Blanca group . . . [from the summit] one of the most magnificent views in all Colorado was spread out before [the party]. The greater portion of Colorado and New Mexico was embraced in this field of vision. This point [Blanca Peak] is the highest in the Sierra Blanca group and, so far as is known at the present time, is the highest in Colorado.

Three views of Mount Lindsay, rising 14,042 feet, less than two miles east of Blanca Peak.

The magnificent Sierra Blanca in the San Luis Valley is one of Colorado's most impressive groups of mountains. From left to right they are: Ellingwood Peak (at extreme right on this page — not an official Fourteener), Blanca Peak and Little Bear Peak (on the opposite page).

BLANCA and
LITTLE BEAR

At that time, Hayden calculated Blanca Peak's elevation as 14,464 feet and felt even further that it "may be regarded as the highest, or at least next to the highest, yet known in the United States."

Blanca Peak's official elevation is 14,345 feet, making it Colorado's fifth highest. In that same 1876 report, one of Hayden's topographers, A. D. Wilson (for whom two Fourteeners are named) also spoke glowingly of Blanca Peak: "[It] is one of the finest geodetic points in all of Colorado, owing to its height, position and sharp, conical form." Wilson also was quick to point out the imperfections in using the barometer as an instrument for measuring heights in a mountainous region, "where local storms and sudden atmospheric changes occur so frequently . . . [making it] very difficult to determine with certainty which is the highest peak." Still, so thorough were Hayden's men that Wilson's assistant "made over 1,000 pages (each 6 by 10 inches) of profile sketches [of the mountains] during the field season of 1875."

Franklin Rhoda (Wilson's half-brother) called the Sierra Blanca "a family of giants, and when you stand on the center peaks you can look over all the others." Rhoda, who was one of the better writers in Hayden's party, made note of a ptarmigan's nest, bear, mountain sheep, elk and "great meadows covered with rich growth of grass and flowers." He was particularly gifted at describing mountains, as exemplified by his report of a "steep, rocky wall of a great cavity marked with many long and curious streaks of snow, which formed a great variety of figures, yet all reaching like fingers down toward the frozen lakes and fields of snow in the bottom of the basin. So high above them rose the walls of rock that the lakes were nearly all day in the shadow."

Mount Lindsey (14,042 feet), north of Fort Garland and east of Blanca Peak, can be seen from U.S. Highway 160. Once known as Old Baldy, it was renamed in 1954 for Malcolm Lindsey, late Denver city attorney from Trinidad,

Colorado, who was an avid climber and leader of youth groups in the Colorado Mountain Club. This club, incidentally, has a membership of more than 5,000, was founded in 1912, and is one of the region's most notable climbing organizations.

Little Bear Peak and Blanca Peak, located north of the town of Blanca on U.S. Highway 160, can be seen from the south and west — from anywhere in the San Luis Valley. A. D. Wilson described the San Luis Valley as "a great plain surrounded by high ranges and lofty peaks, bounded on the west and northwest by the San Juan and Sawatch ranges, on the east and northeast by the Sangre de Cristo Range, and on the south by a succession of volcanic buttes."

Little Bear Peak is connected to Mount Blanca by a precarious and spectacular 1½-mile long knife-edge ridge. Blanca is a Spanish name for "white," and the peak was so named, no doubt, for the year-round snow on its summit.

Another spur of Blanca Peak is Ellingwood

*F*lying easterly past Sierra Blanca, you can see Ellingwood Peak to the left of Little Bear Peak . . .

. . . a few miles farther east, Ellingwood is no longer visible, but Blanca Peak can be seen to the right of Little Bear Peak . . .

Peak, one of a half-dozen so-called "Forgotten Fourteeners." Ellingwood's elevation is 14,042 feet, but it is not an official member of the exclusive club.

Let's explain: Surveyors, with their fancy instruments nowadays, can come pretty close to establishing the elevation of Colorado's peaks. They do this every few years to, among other reasons, help others analyze weather phenomena. But many times nature can fool the instruments (as it did Hayden's men). Aerial cameras (which Hayden didn't have), one of the more exact ways to determine elevations, can often be tricked by shadows crossing the peaks, thus probably accounting for some of the statistical changes over the years.

Now, under U.S. Geological Survey regulations, a mountain, to qualify for the Over-14,000-foot Club, must be at least 500 feet taller than the "saddle" connecting it with another peak. A "saddle" is the lowest point between two peaks. Ellingwood Peak does not qualify because its crest (14,042 feet) is only 352 feet higher than the saddle (13,690 feet) connecting it to Blanca Peak. Blanca qualifies easily, as it is 655 feet higher than the saddle.

Under these rules, Little Bear Peak should not be an official Fourteener. Its elevation (14,037) is 377 feet higher than the saddle (13,660) between it and Blanca Peak. In reality, then, Little Bear is a

. . . and now — due south — you can see to the north (from left) Little Bear Peak, Ellingwood Peak and Blanca Peak.

BLANCA and LITTLE BEAR

BLANCA

Blanca Peak is the most prominent mountain in this air view of Sierra Blanca, looking toward the southwest.

21

ear the Great Sand Dunes National Monument on Colorado Highway 150, looking northwardly, you can see (from left) Kit Carson Mountain, Crestone Peak and Crestone Needle.

KIT CARSON, CRESTONE NEEDLE, CRESTONE PEAK, HUMBOLDT

part of Blanca. But, Little Bear has been considered one of Colorado's Fourteeners so long that nobody has had the heart to not include it on the maps. In this case, once a charter member, always a member.

What this all means is that while there are a number of peaks in Colorado higher than 14,000 feet, only 53 officially belong to the exclusive club. And, as long as there are mountains there will be photographers to remind us how beautiful they are. In that respect, then, statistics don't mean a thing.

Ellingwood Peak was named for Albert R. Ellingwood, a Colorado Mountain Club pioneer who was among the first to climb all Fourteeners. Other pioneers of Colorado mountaineering include Herman Buhl and Carl Blaurock. Blaurock and William Ervin in 1923, with the ascent of Kit Carson Mountain, became the first to climb all 46 recognized Fourteeners at that time. Blaurock later climbed each Fourteener as it was added to the list, and, in the summer of 1973, marked his 64th year of climbing by hiking up 13,734-foot Notch Mountain in the Sawatch Range. Author William M. Bueler says that without question, Blaurock's climbing career is the longest in Colorado.

Northwest of the Sierra Blanca is the popular Great Sand Dunes National Monument, which is reachable by a couple of routes from Alamosa. North of the Sand Dunes are the other Fourteeners in the Sangre de Cristo Range — Kit Carson Mountain, Crestone Peak, Crestone Needle and Humboldt Peak. Kit Carson (14,165 feet), western peak of this group and named for the famous scout, is due east of the town of Crestone, which is east of Colorado Highway 17. From this highway, or from the road to the Great Sand Dunes National Monument, you can view the Crestone mountains, which are southeast of Kit Carson Mountain. "Creston" is Spanish for "cockscomb," which probably accounts for the naming of the jagged Crestones. Crestone Peak, at 14,294 feet, is one of Colorado's higher mountains (Number 7).

Although Humboldt Peak (14,064 feet) is close to the Crestones (just to the east of them), it is best viewed from the other side of the range, in the Wet Mountain Valley near Westcliffe, on Colorado Highway 69. According to *The Fourteeners*, a book by Perry Eberhart and Philip Schmuck: German settlers in the Wet Mountain Valley probably named the peak for Alexander von Humboldt, a geographer and world climber.

*O*n the following pages, an air view shows Kit Carson Mountain to the far left, with Crestone Peak, Crestone Needle and Humboldt Peak pictured on the right-hand page.

*S*een from the Wet Mountain Valley side are, from left, Humboldt Peak, Crestone Needle and Crestone Peak.

Section Two . . .

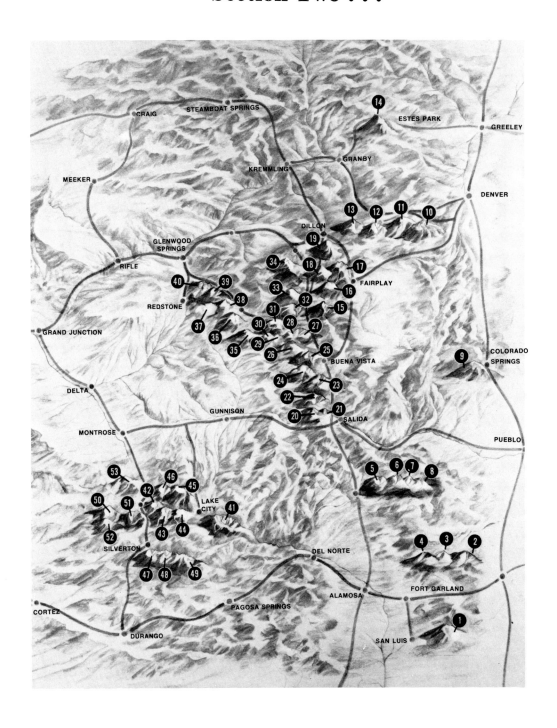

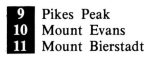

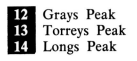

9	Pikes Peak	**12**	Grays Peak
10	Mount Evans	**13**	Torreys Peak
11	Mount Bierstadt	**14**	Longs Peak

Front Range

Pikes Peak stands like a huge watchtower fronting the plains.

Gustavus R. Bechler, Hayden Survey, 1875

F. V. Hayden and his men, of course, were not the only ones surveying Colorado in the 19th Century and reporting to the people back East of this great and grand area. The quest for knowledge about the West following the Civil War prompted four geographical and geological surveys from 1867 to 1879. As explained in Richard A. Bartlett's book, *Great Surveys of the American West*, two of these explorations were under the administration of the War Department — one headed by a civilian, Clarence King, and the other by Lt. George Montague Wheeler. Wheeler, like Hayden, climbed many Fourteeners, some for the first time, and the two men often worked the same range at the same time. The other two great surveys of the West were under the administration of the Department of the Interior — one led by Hayden and the other by John Wesley Powell.

Powell, a one-armed Civil War major and Illinois geology professor, discovered "truths" of the West by floating down the Colorado River. He climbed Pikes Peak on July 26, 1867, with a group that included his wife, Emma Dean. She was the fourth woman to reach the summit (the first woman was Mrs. Julia Archibald Holmes of Kansas, on August 5, 1858). In the summer of 1868 (on August 23), Powell was the first to climb another Front Range mountain, Longs Peak. He found a way up on the Estes Park side of the peak. Mount Powell (about 500 feet short of being a Fourteener) in the Gore Range was named for him.

Powell, of course, was not the first to climb Pikes Peak — neither was Hayden (though one of his men wrote of a bitterly cold snow storm he encountered on the summit), nor Wheeler, nor — for that matter — the man for whom the peak was named. An expedition in 1820, led by Major Stephen H. Long, climbed it and named it for a botanist in the party, Dr. Edwin James. "James Peak" later was named for the first white man who told the world about it, Zebulon Montgomery Pike. Pike was an American explorer and soldier who, seven years after he spotted his peak, was killed in the War of 1812.

Pike, in his Southwestern Expedition of 1806, "one of exploration and conciliation of the Indian tribes," moved up the Arkansas to the site of the present city of Pueblo. From his camp there, on November 15, he sighted the peak. As he wrote:

At two o'clock in the afternoon I thought I could distinguish a mountain to our right, which appeared like a small blue cloud; viewed it with the spy glass, and was still more confirmed in my conjecture . . . in half an hour, they [the Rocky Mountains] appeared in full view before us.

Pike and two of his soldiers hoped to arrive at the foot of the mountain by evening. The distance from Pueblo to the peak is about 50 miles, and indicates how badly Pike was fooled by the rarefied atmosphere. By darkness, Pike had covered only a fourth of the distance. After spending a week attempting to scale the peak, he concluded that "no human being could have ascended to its pinnacle."

One of Hayden's men, Dr. A. C. Peale, a geologist in the exploration of the South Park in 1873, wrote about "the Garden of the Gods, the springs and the various beautiful canyons about the foot of Pikes Peak." Then he made a very true observation: "It is to their attraction, perhaps, that Colorado Springs and the village of Manitou owe their prosperity."

Colorado Springs lies almost in the shadow of 14,110-foot Pikes Peak, which, though not the highest, has become the most famous mountain in Colorado. People have run up it; hiked up it; roared up it in race cars or driven up it leisurely in automobiles; zoomed up it on motorcycles; gone up it in buses or in the famous "cog" trains of the Manitou & Pikes Peak Railway. Begun in the late 19th Century, the train — which is operated by a privately owned railway company — slowly winds its way 8.9 miles up the north and east slopes of the peak. A fine panoramic view awaits visitors at the summit, where even in summer a snow shower is not unusual. The "Cog Wheel Route" is the

PIKES

*P*ikes Peak, Colorado's most famous mountain, is seen here from the Garden of the Gods.

Pikes Peak hovers over Colorado Springs (above). On the opposite page, the mountain takes on a red glow in this view at sunset from Colorado Highway 67 near Cripple Creek.

highest railroad in the United States and the highest rack-and-pinion "cog" railway in the world.

One novel event that has taken place atop Pikes Peak since the early 1920s is the shooting of fireworks on New Year's Eve by the Colorado Springs AdAmAn Club. Each December 31 the club initiates one new member (it "adds a man") by climbing the mountain and welcoming in the New Year with a fireworks display.

The area made famous by the peak that Zebulon Pike felt no man would climb includes such widely known landmarks and tourist attractions as the Garden of the Gods, Manitou Springs, the Air Force Academy, Cheyenne Mountain (with a zoo and the Will Rogers Shrine along its slopes, and a big cave within it that houses NORAD, the military nerve center of North America), a number of other military installations, and the Broadmoor Hotel.

About 60 air miles northwest of Pikes Peak is another popular Fourteener, 14,264-foot Mount Evans. Named for John Evans, Colorado's second territorial governor, the mountain is southwest of Idaho Springs, off Interstate 70. Colorado Highway 103 takes you to scenic Echo Lake, from where it is 14 miles to the summit. Through the years, many scientific experiments have been conducted from Mount Evans. A couple of artists, one being Albert Bierstadt for whom another Front Range Fourteener is named, climbed it first in the early 1860s.

The often-repeated statement that the road up Mount Evans is the "highest automobile road in the world" may not be correct. In a letter to *Empire Magazine*, C. William Keighin of Denver explains:

There is a road from Lima, Peru, South America, into the central Andes [the Trans-Andean Highway] which, at Ticlio — the highest point — is approximately 15,800 feet above sea level. When we were in Peru, I drove on another road which reached approximately 16,400 feet, but this was not quite a regularly traveled road [it led to a mine which operated off and on]. The road over Ticlio was being paved while we were working in Peru [1960-'63]; at the rate the work was progressing, they still may be paving it. It was, however, the main — and almost only — link between the coast and the interior.

Mount Evans was the last of the Fourteeners in Colorado climbed by Steve Boyer in the summer of 1976. Boyer, then 29 years old and a student at the University of Colorado School of Medicine, climbed all 53 Fourteeners (plus "orphan" Ellingwood Peak) in the fantastic time of 21 days, 3 hours and 20 minutes. Boyer started his endurance feat in the Needle Mountains of the San Juan Range with Gary Tiller, then a 25-year-old graduate student at the University of Denver. Tiller, however, did not finish all of the climbs. Boyer ascended the last nine Fourteeners — including Grays, Torreys, Bierstadt and Evans in the Front Range — during a 26-hour period that began at

EVANS

5:15 in the morning. He walked almost 300 miles, climbed some 147,000 feet in altitude, and drove 2,000 miles across the state.

Climbing all of the Fourteeners has been accomplished by several mountain enthusiasts, but Jack Eggleston of Denver claims to have climbed all 53 peaks more times than anyone else. He first reached all 53 at the age of 17 in 1957; he finished climbing them all for the second time in 1963; wound up the third round in 1969, and was in the process of ascending some of them for the fourth time at this writing. He started climbing mountains at the age of 10 with his father, William Eggleston, a retired schoolteacher who had climbed 42 of the 53.

Why does Jack Eggleston climb? Not necessarily "because it's there," but "because of the view from the top, the satisfaction of reaching a goal and the opportunity to enjoy the wilderness and nature." He also has climbed other well-known peaks outside of Colorado — the Grand Teton in Wyoming twice and four Fourteeners in California, including Mount Whitney. Whitney is the highest peak in the contiguous United States at 14,495 feet (Mount McKinley in Alaska is the highest in North America at 20,320 feet; Mount Aconcagua in Argentina is the highest in South America at 22,834 feet; while Mount Everest in Nepal-Tibet, Asia, tops them all with an elevation of 29,028 feet). Eggleston was one of the youngest climbers (at age 13) to reach the summit of 14,410-foot Mount Rainier in Washington state with his father in 1953. On a trip to Europe in 1968, he climbed the Matterhorn.

EVANS

*W*ell-known to tourists, Mount Evans is Colorado's 14th highest peak, enjoyed by both mountain travelers (opposite page) and city dwellers from downtown Denver.

Getting back to Colorado's Fourteeners along the Front Range, Mount Bierstadt (14,060 feet) is west of Mount Evans and can be viewed from Guanella Pass between Georgetown and Grant. This mountain was named for the 19th-Century artist who specialized in romantic paintings of peaks. A peak called Rosalie, which rises 13,575 feet south of Mount Evans, was named for Bierstadt's wife.

Grays Peak is south of Interstate 70 and can be seen from Bakersville, west of Georgetown. Just northwest of Grays is Torreys Peak. Both are northwest of Mount Bierstadt and both were named by botanist Charles Christopher Parry, who climbed many Front Range mountains. Parry named them for well-known 19th-Century botany professors at Ivy League schools, Asa Gray and John Torrey. The Indians referred to the peaks as "Ant Hills"; the mountains also have been known as "Twins," because of their almost-equal height (Grays Peak at 14,270 feet is three feet higher than Torreys Peak).

Mount Bierstadt as seen from Guanella Pass (opposite page) and from the air looking northeast (above). Bierstadt and surrounding peaks once were called the Chicago Mountains.

BIERSTADT

In 1875 Gustavus R. Bechler, a topographer for the Hayden Survey, wrote that Grays and Torreys "stand in the center of bold, rich and varied mountain scenery." Earlier in his report, Bechler was inspired to comment on the beautiful setting of Longs Peak:

> To the north of Longs Peak and 6,000 feet beneath its lofty summit lies that beautiful valley area called Estes Park, with a chain of huge mountains and peaks encircling it on nearly all sides in a grand amphitheatrical shape ... The bold and weather-beaten appearance [of the mountains] adds much to the impressiveness and magnificence of the scenery.

Longs Peak was named for Major Stephen H. Long, who saw it from the eastern plains in 1820, but did not climb it; the first recorded ascent, as we mentioned earlier, was by Major Powell (his party included William N. Byers, editor of *The Rocky Mountain News*) in 1868. Several historians have pointed out that Indians earlier had an eagle trap on the summit.

This great mountain, with its steep and perpendicular faces, has claimed numerous lives since the 1860s. At an elevation of 14,255 feet, Longs Peak is Colorado's 15th highest and the tallest point in Rocky Mountain National Park. It can be viewed from Longmont or Loveland, just west of Interstate 25, or close up from Colorado Highway 7 from Lyons to Estes Park. The back side can be seen from the scenic Trail Ridge Road.

Longs Peak, which was a major training ground for climbers in the successful 1963 American Mount Everest expedition, has a commanding position in the Front Range. From the summit you can look down on Pikes Peak to the south, into Kansas and Nebraska in the east, to the Flattops beyond the Colorado River westward and north to Wyoming's Medicine Bow Range.

GRAYS

Grays Peak, as seen from Interstate 70 at Bakersville, is Colorado's ninth highest.

The peak has been climbed thousands of times, but several (maybe as many as three dozen) persons attempting to scale it have died by falls, exposure, lightning or exhaustion. The skull of one climber was found nearly 20 years after he had disappeared on the lower approaches to the east face. At one point on the east face, there is a virtually free drop of 1,675 feet. Still, several routes, especially on the north, are relatively easily climbed. In 1931, a one-legged man from Nebraska made it to the summit on crutches; four years earlier, a couple was married on top during a snowstorm. And in 1880, a half-dozen members of the Longmont Cornet Band gave a concert on the summit.

Cal Queal of Crested Butte, Colorado, in his February 22, 1970, *Empire Magazine* story about how one climber survived the fall and midwinter cold of the mountain, wrote a fitting tribute to Longs Peak: "It is not merely high and immense. Its moods seem to change constantly with the passage of the sun from one horizon to the other; with the coming and going of almost perpetual storms, with the seasons. It is a challenging, spectacular peak, distinctive in a kind of personal way to anyone who has a feeling for mountains."

TORREYS

Torreys Peak also is visible from Interstate 70 at Bakersville. It and Grays were called "Ant Hills" by the Indians.

41

The east face (left) of Longs Peak has claimed the lives of many climbers. Tourists get a magnificent view of the mountain from scenic Trail Ridge Road (below).

LONGS

LONGS

This view, looking west, of Longs Peak is from near Colorado Highway 7. The peak is the highest point in Rocky Mountain National Park.

F. V. HAYDEN had a great "feel" for the mountains.

JOHN WESLEY POWELL was the first to climb Longs Peak.

Hayden and his men, as we have noted, had a great "feel" for the mountains and they wrote with fascination, respect and awe:

> The remarkably rounded and grassy appearance of these high mountain ranges in many instances is quite surprising, and we ask how so great a thickness of superficial earth could have accumulated so far above timberline.

The "grassy meadows, flowers and beauty of aspen trees at any season" all were a part of this great scene that unfolded before them. Insects, too, held the attention of the survey men. In the 1873 report, for instance, Lt. W. L. Carpenter wrote: "Spiders appeared to thrive best [of any insect]; being always present at all elevations, and apparently indifferent to climate."

Carpenter felt that the "barrier presented by the mountains is of great benefit to the agricultural interest of Colorado." He elaborated:

> It is safe to estimate that not more than one-tenth of the number [of grasshoppers] which rise from the plains and valleys of Utah ever succeed in crossing [the Continental Divide] . . . Myriads of grasshoppers swarm from the Pacific slope in July and August, and . . . are arrested by high peaks and ridges of the Rocky Mountains and, becoming benumbed by cold, drop down to perish.

45

LONGS

Rocky Mountain Bighorn Sheep (above) call the high country their home. A trail (right) in Rocky Mountain National Park offers this view of Longs Peak.

Section Three . . .

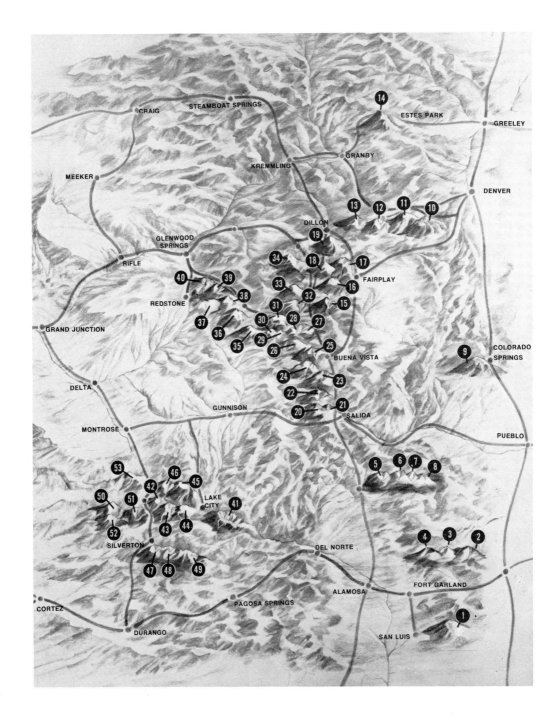

15	Mount Sherman
16	Mount Bross
17	Mount Lincoln
18	Mount Democrat
19	Quandary Peak

Mosquito and Tenmile Ranges

Scenes of great beauty meet the eye at every step, and yet the area is so large that we must have left unseen . . . views of even greater beauty and value.

F. V. Hayden, 1873

One of the most frustrating things that Hayden and his men encountered when reaching the summit of a mountain was finding indications that someone else already had been there. It was downright frustrating to think, while they were climbing, that they were the first to ascend the peak only to learn that the honor already had been bestowed inconspicuously on an Indian who had set an eagle trap, or a prospector who celebrated the occasion by emptying a whisky bottle — or maybe a frolicking bear completely oblivious to the prestige the white men were attaching to "getting there first."

Franklin Rhoda of the Hayden Survey team expressed it eloquently:

When you feel you are treading a path never trod by a living thing before, and your imagination begins to build for itself a romantic picture, if some such vile, worldly thing as a paper collar or a whisky bottle does not intrude itself on the sight, some beastly quadruped . . . break[s] the precious solitude and scatter[s] your airy castle to the winds.

The Hayden men would become so annoyed at a grizzly bear romping past them that they would throw rocks at it long after it had disappeared. And it was out of pure perturbation that they named a peak in the Needle Mountains of southwestern Colorado for the large, heavy mammal with the long, shaggy hair — Mount Oso (the Spanish name for "bear"). Its elevation is 13,706 feet.

Many men and women, as we have mentioned, have succeeded in climbing Fourteeners, with or without the presence of bears, but probably the most remarkable accomplishment was the ascending of all 67 peaks over 14,000 feet in the contiguous United States in 48 days by George Smith of Aurora, Colorado, and his four sons. The "Climbing Smiths" — including Flint, then 22, Quade, 18, Cody, 17, and Tyle, 15 — recorded this feat in the summer of 1974, setting out for Longs Peak on the Fourth of July. In all, they drove 4,000 miles, climbed and walked more than 500 miles

and some 215,000 feet vertically. They climbed all of Colorado's Fourteeners in 33 days; spent two days driving to California, climbed the 13 peaks there in 11 days, then went to Washington state where they reached the top of Mount Rainier on the 48th day. Their strategy was simple: "Climb one peak and head for the next."

The youngest son, Tyle, was 6 years old when he climbed his first Fourteener, 14,036-foot Mount Sherman in the Mosquito Range. By July of 1968, when Tyle was 8, the Smiths had climbed all 53 in Colorado. A year later they became five of only 16 climbers to have ascended all 67 Fourteeners.

The elder Smith's accomplishments are even more remarkable when you consider that his right

Mount Sherman features a natural amphitheatre at the foot of the peak (above). The view of Sherman on the opposite page is from a mining road east of Leadville.

SHERMAN

arm was mangled in an automobile accident when he was 4 years old, leaving the elbow frozen at a right angle with no wrist movement and resulting. in the loss of the thumb and forefinger.

George Smith introduced his sons to the Fourteeners by having them climb Mount Sherman, whose gentle slopes make it one of the easiest (and most popular for family outings) to ascend. The peak, named for Civil War General William T. Sherman, is west of Fairplay and can be seen best from the road heading east from Leadville to the Mount Sherman mine.

Another Mosquito Range Fourteener — Mount Democrat, northwest of Fairplay — is of special significance to Smith and his wife, Marilou. Their honeymoon trip, after a visit to Wyoming's Tetons, included a climb to the top of 14,148-foot Democrat. It was named by Southerners during the Civil War and can be seen from Colorado Highway 9 on Fremont Pass.

BROSS

M̄ount Bross, 22nd highest in Colorado as seen from different locations on the south side of Hoosier Pass.

East of Mount Democrat is Colorado's eighth highest, 14,286-foot Mount Lincoln, which greatly impressed Hayden. In his 1873 report, he wrote:

> The view from the summit of Mount Lincoln is wonderful in its extent . . . [from its top] probably there is no portion of the world, accessible to the traveling public, where such a wilderness of lofty peaks can be seen within a single scope of vision.

Mount Lincoln is the highest in the Mosquito Range, which runs south from west of Hoosier Pass some 35 miles to Trout Creek Pass on U. S. Highway 24. (According to legend, as retold by author Robert Ormes, the range was named after a mosquito landed on a blank space left for a name on a legal document.) Mount Lincoln, which can be viewed from the top of Hoosier Pass on Colorado Highway 9, was popular with early day

LINCOLN

A skiff of snow swirls atop Mount Lincoln in the view at left from a lookout point on Hoosier Pass. The photo at right is an aerial view of Lincoln, which was one of the favorite mountains of early-day prospectors. They named it for the 16th President of the United States.

prospectors. Had environmentalists been active in those days, they no doubt would have been critical of the "defacing" done by the prospectors. The mountain yielded millions of dollars in gold and silver, but not before suffering considerable pockmarks from the miners' diggings. The mountain also was a recreation outlet for the prospectors, who enjoyed racing each other up and down its slopes. The miners named it for the 16th President of the United States, and its elevation at one time was estimated as high as 18,000 feet. Considered a part of Mount Lincoln is another "orphaned" Fourteener — 14,238-foot Mount Cameron.

The other Fourteener in the Mosquito Range, 14,172-foot Mount Bross, is south of Mount Lincoln and also can be seen to the west from Hoosier Pass between Fairplay and Breckenridge. It was named for William Bross, a lieutenant governor of Illinois in the late 1860s. He visited Colorado frequently and had more than a passing interest in mining and railroads.

DEMOCRAT

The photo below of Mount Democrat was taken from the ground, looking southeast across railroad tracks. The photo on the opposite page offers almost the same view from the air.

QUANDARY

*Q*uandary Peak was another mountain that was very popular with early miners. Here are three views of Quandary, including one from the air (left) that looks toward the southwest, up McCullough Gulch.

Continuing northward, but still south of Interstate 70, is the Tenmile Range of which Quandary Peak is the lone Fourteener. It is the 13th highest in the state at 14,265 feet. To the west of Quandary runs Tenmile Creek, which, according to Gustavus R. Bechler of the Hayden Survey, got its name "from the supposed distance which it, at its intersection with the Blue River, was supposed to be from the mining town of Breckenridge."

How did Quandary get its name? According to one story, early day miners were in a dilemma — or "quandary" — to identify some rocks found near the mountain's summit. The mountain can be seen from the north side of Hoosier Pass.

While, as we explained earlier in this chapter, Hayden and his men were frustrated by the presence of grizzly bears, they were able to reap some benefits from these animals. The surveyors often were able to hike better in the snow by stepping in the tracks of the bears.

Hayden's journals also mention seeing antelope, elk, deer, mountain lions, rabbits, beavers and skunks. But it was a four-legged creature — the mule — the men brought with them that played a big role in the explorations. Even though, as author Richard A. Bartlett explains, the mule was prone to spook, often would rub its rider against rocks and trees — and at times would become so exhausted (and probably disgusted at traveling 20 miles a day) that it would jump into water to drown — it was surefooted. And that, as so many climbers have experienced, was very important.

Section Four . . .

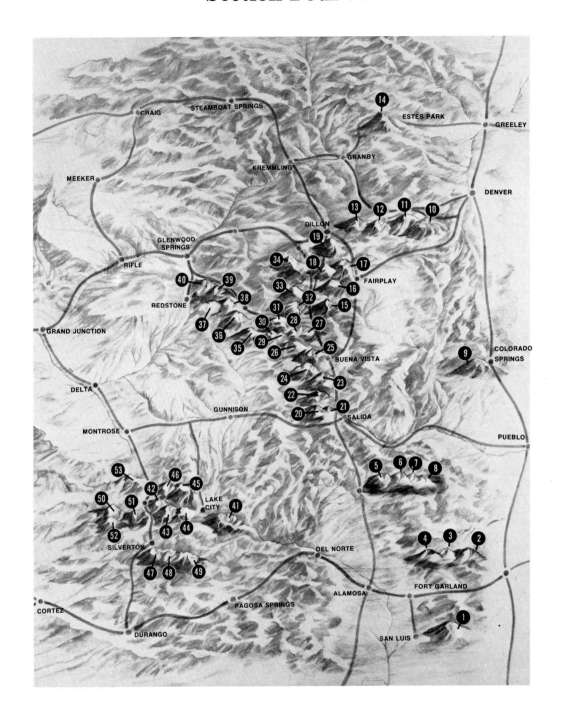

20	Tabeguache Mountain	25	Mount Columbia	30	Huron Peak
21	Mount Shavano	26	Mount Harvard	31	La Plata Peak
22	Mount Antero	27	Mount Oxford	32	Mount Elbert
23	Mount Princeton	28	Mount Belford	33	Mount Massive
24	Mount Yale	29	Missouri Mountain	34	Mount of the Holy Cross

Sawatch Range

. . . a remarkable range of mountains, the Sawatch, which, with its lofty peaks . . . looms up like a massive wall, with a wilderness of conical peaks along its summits.

F. V. Hayden, 1873

Geology and the natural sciences were Hayden's all-consuming passion, and he worked so rapidly and published so quickly that, as author Richard A. Bartlett explains, "shoddiness became the hallmark of his reports." In many respects, Hayden's reports are boring reading. Yet, lest we forget or ignore the immense importance of his work, it was through the journalists and photographers — like William Henry Jackson — who accompanied his expeditions that the Hayden Survey popularized the wonders of the West. And Hayden himself, even though working at a brisk pace, found time to record his romantic feelings for and impressions of the mountain ranges he and his men were working. His 1874 report included this statement:

> The Sawatch group is one of the loftiest and most symmetrical ranges in the West. It extends from Mount of the Holy Cross to the north, southward to the San Luis Valley, a distance of over 80 miles. For this entire distance, the range literally bristles with lofty points. The uniformity of this great mountain mass is a remarkable feature. Standing on some high peak and glancing along its pointed summits from north to south, there seems to be comparatively little variation either in form or height.

Hayden felt the Sawatch Range was one of the grandest eruptive masses on the continent. He wrote of the "tremendous effects of erosion, remarkable upthrusts of igneous material, eruptive groups [which have] thrown the sedimentary beds into utmost confusion, producing remarkable faults and irregularities."

The Sawatch Range, from an Indian word for "water of the blue earth" (probably referring to the lake that once covered the San Luis Valley), contains 15 Fourteeners, including the four highest and five of the top 10. From south to north are such notables as Mount Antero, 10th highest and a crystal-hunter's paradise; Mount Harvard, just one foot from being No. 2; La Plata Peak, No. 4; Mount Elbert and Mount Massive, the two highest in Colorado. And the range's northernmost Fourteener, Mount of the Holy Cross, though just barely a member of Colorado's Highest Club at 14,005 feet, achieved worldwide fame after William H. Jackson first photographed it in 1873. Then,

Thomas Moran painted it in 1874 and Henry Wadsworth Longfellow was inspired by a picture of it in 1879 to write a poem relating to his wife who had been dead for 18 years. Though Mount of the Holy Cross today is probably the least climbed and most isolated of Colorado's Fourteeners, a series of pilgrimages to its vicinity from post-World War I to the mid-1930s also focused global attention upon it. In the summer of 1976 there were faint indications that pilgrimages might be resumed, though probably not of the magnitude of the earlier ones. But, more about this later.

At the southern end of the Sawatch Range are three Fourteeners whose names are of Indian origin: Tabeguache, Shavano and Antero. Tabeguache Mountain (14,155 feet) is connected to and northwest of Shavano Peak (separated by a mile of easy walking), and can be seen from U.S. Highway 50 on the east side of Monarch Pass. Tabeguache was named for a band of Ute Indians which once roamed the area. Shavano Peak was named for the band's war chief, Che-Wa-No. The head chief was the famous Ouray; a mountain is named for him, but it is 29 feet shy of being a Fourteener.

The photo on the opposite page offers a bird's-eye view of Tabeguache Mountain (to the left) and Mount Shavano (right), looking north. The photo above of Tabeguache was taken from Monarch Pass.

TABEGUACHE and SHAVANO

Shavano Peak (14,229 feet), which can be viewed best from U.S. Highway 285 north of Poncha Springs, is noted for the "snow angel" on its east side. Snow in crevices forms a figure with outstretched arms; it is in best shape in early July, but can usually be seen most of the summer. According to one legend, Chief Che-Wa-No prayed at the mountain for the soul of his dying friend, Jim Beckwourth, the black scout who was fatally injured in a riding accident in 1853. Since that time, the story goes, the "Angel of Shavano" has returned each spring to indicate that the Indian's prayers have been answered.

The nearby ghost town of Shavano prospered as a mining community in the early 1880s.

Zebulon Pike and his men ate Christmas dinner in 1806 near the base of 14,269-foot Mount Antero, which is north of Tabeguache and south of Mount Princeton (it can be seen looking west from U.S. Highway 285). Antero was named for a Ute chief who worked with Che-Wa-No in trying to bring peace between the whites and Indians.

Just below Mount Antero's summit is the highest important mineral-collecting field in North America. The mountain yields such crystals as smoky

If you look closely at the photo on the opposite page of Mount Shavano, you will see a figure with outstretched arms formed by snow in the deep crevices. This is the legendary Snow Angel, or Angel of Shavano; the view is just off U.S. Highway 285, looking northwest. The Snow Angel also is visible in the aerial photo above.

SHAVANO

The view at right is how a bird would see Mount Antero, looking toward the west. Colorado's 10th highest peak is a haven for rockhounds, and the scene at the left is near the summit. The photo below shows the four-wheel-drive road that leads to the crystal area.

ANTERO

and clear quartz, flourite, beryl, phenakite, mica and aquamarine, the latter being discovered in the mid-1880s by Nathaniel D. Wanamaker. He built a small stone cabin about 800 feet below the mountain top. Edwin J. Over, Jr. of Pueblo, Colorado, explored the mountain in the 1920s and 1930s, and is considered to have been one of the mountain's most successful crystal hunters.

Just south of the summit, some members of the Colorado Mineral Society, in 1949, erected a bronze plaque with this inscription: "Mount Antero Mineral Park — World Famous Locality for Superb Crystals of Aquamarine-Phenakite-Bertrandite."

North of these "Indian peaks" are five Fourteeners known as the Collegiate Peaks: Princeton, Yale, Harvard, Columbia and Oxford.

Mount Princeton (14,197 feet) — south of Cottonwood Pass and separated from Mount

THE HAYDEN SURVEY MEN found their mules surefooted, though stubborn and unpredictable at times.

PRINCETON

*M*ount Princeton, as seen from U.S. Highway 285, near Chalk Creek. Princeton once was known as Chalk Mountain because of its white chalk cliffs.

Antero by Chalk Creek — also can be seen from U.S. Highway 285 and reached by way of the road to St. Elmo (Colorado Highway 162 part way, west of Nathrop). Treasure hunters long have searched the cliffs of Mount Princeton for — according to legend — valuable Indian trinkets buried there some 200 years ago by Spanish conquistadores. Prospectors and miners, however, have had better luck, as the mountain was the site of one of the area's first rich silver-producing mines, the Hortense. Mount Princeton was first climbed, according to records, on July 17, 1877, by William Libbey, Jr. Named after the Princeton University Scientific Expedition of that year, it once was called "Chalk Mountain" by the George M. Wheeler Survey because of its white chalk cliffs of a crumbly rock known as quartz monzonite.

Henry Gannett, who later would serve as a valuable topographer for Hayden's Survey and become known as the "father of American map-making," was among Harvard University's first mining school graduates to explore Colorado's mountains with Prof. J. D. Whitney in 1869. Whitney, a graduate of Yale and a surveyor of California, named 14,196-foot Mount Yale and also Mount Harvard.

PRINCETON

*O*n *the opposite page, you can pick out Mount Princeton, looking west from the air. In the ground view below, Princeton is visible looking west from near the junction of U.S. Highways 24-285.*

YALE

*M*ount Yale, Colorado's 21st highest mountain — north of Princeton — is seen in this view from Chalk Creek, looking to the northwest.

74

The two other peaks of the Sawatch's Collegiate Range were named by members of the Colorado Mountain Club. In 1916, while he was putting club registers on the peaks, Roger Toll named 14,073-foot Mount Columbia; Mount Oxford, surveyed but apparently not climbed by Hayden, was named by a Rhodes Scholar from Denver, Jerry Hart.

Both Mount Yale (which is north of Mount Princeton on the other side of Cottonwood Pass and west of Buena Vista) and Mount Columbia (which is north of Yale, southeast of Harvard and connected to it by a jagged ridge) can be seen from U.S. Highways 285-24. Mount Harvard, Colorado's third-highest at 14,420 feet, can be viewed from U.S. Highway 24 (although the peak is hard to pick out).

Mount Oxford, whose gentle slopes make it a popular family climb, is on the eastern end of a long ridge that also includes Mount Belford and Missouri Mountain. These mountains run west along Clear Creek, but their summits cannot be seen from the nearby valley.

Mount Belford, west of Oxford, was named for a colorful, early Colorado politician, Judge James Belford. His red hair and flamboyant mannerisms earned him the nickname "Red-Headed Rooster of the Rockies." Ironically, the mountain named for him is relatively drab and uninspiring.

Missouri Mountain is just southwest of Belford and connected by ridges to Oxford and Harvard. Huron Peak, west of Missouri, can be seen best from an airplane. Huron qualified for the Four-

COLUMBIA

A jagged ridge connects Mount Columbia and Mount Harvard, northwest of Buena Vista. On the opposite page is a ground view of Columbia, while in the aerial view (below), you are looking toward the northeast.

HARVARD

*M*ount Harvard is difficult to pick out from the ground, but this aerial view clearly shows its dominant position among the neighboring peaks.

Looking south across the Clear Creek drainage in the aerial photo above are, from left: Mount Oxford, Mount Belford and Missouri Mountain, southwest of Leadville. The photo on the opposite page shows the gentle slopes of Oxford, once a forgotten Fourteener.

teeners Club by a mere five feet; it is the 51st highest in Colorado at 14,005 feet, the same elevation as Mount of the Holy Cross.

Oxford, Belford and Missouri have been significant because of their relative oblivion for so many years. For instance, Mount Oxford, now ranked 27th in the state with an elevation of 14,153 feet, was surveyed by Hayden in 1873, but it wasn't until the mid-1920s that it was officially recognized as a Fourteener. Mount Belford, No. 19 at 14,197 feet, was long considered a part of Mount Oxford

OXFORD, BELFORD, MISSOURI

U. S. Geological Survey

ONCE ATOP a mountain a century ago, members of the Hayden party would spend several hours surveying, mapping and sketching the surrounding peaks.

HURON

and only in recent years was it afforded a name, that of orator Belford, who also was Colorado's first elected U. S. representative. Missouri Mountain received its own identity in the 1950s by the Geological Survey. It is 36th highest at 14,067 feet.

North and west of these mountains, and south of Independence Pass (Colorado Highway 82) from where it can be seen, is La Plata Peak. The fourth-highest in Colorado at 14,336 feet, La Plata reportedly was named by the Hayden Survey (the peak's name is Spanish for "silver"). It has been called one of the most satisfying mountains to climb.

La Plata Peak is not to be confused with a group of mountains of the same name, located northwest of Durango near the San Juans in southwestern Colorado.

North of La Plata Peak and separated by Independence Pass is Colorado's No. 1 Fourteener, 14,433-foot Mount Elbert, which is a pretty mountain, but lacking in character. It is best seen from U.S. Highway 24, between Granite and Leadville. Mount Massive, the state's second highest, is just north of Elbert and west of Leadville; it also can be viewed from U.S. Highway 24.

Controversy long has surrounded these two mountains. Through the years, various groups have

Huron Peak, southwest of the ghost town of Vicksburg, is the 51st highest in the state. The aerial photo of Huron on the opposite page was taken from the east.

LA PLATA

La Plata Peak is separated from Mount Elbert — the tallest mountain in Colorado — by Independence Pass, to the north. And, even though Elbert holds the lofty distinction, La Plata Peak is considered to be more impressive. In the ground view of La Plata (above) the camera was aimed toward the southeast, while from the air (right) you are looking southwest. The photo at upper right was taken from Independence Pass.

threatened to construct rock towers atop Mount Massive to give it the few extra feet needed to surpass Elbert. But Elbert remains the highest, while Massive, whose impressive features earned it its name, is No. 2 at 14,421 feet — a foot higher than Mount Harvard. Henry Gannett, then with the Hayden Survey, climbed Mount Massive first in 1874. Attempts failed in later years to name Massive for Gannett (and also for Winston Churchill).

Mount Elbert, named for Samuel Elbert, who was a territorial governor (1873-'74) and married the daughter of second Territorial Governor John Evans, is smooth enough to be climbed all the way on skis. Records indicate that H. W. Stuckle was the first to climb it, in 1874.

Southwest of Mount Elbert is Grizzly Peak, once rated a Fourteener and still afforded that honor in some almanacs. Due west of La Plata Peak, Grizzly now has an official elevation of a few feet less than 14,000.

The prestigious Mount of the Holy Cross, farthest north of the Sawatch Range, is southwest of Redcliff and can be seen at a distance from Colorado Highway 91 north of Fremont Pass looking to the northwest. By automobile, the mountain and its snowy-cross formation can be viewed from the Shrine Pass road between Vail Pass and Redcliff. But the best view is from Notch Mountain, from where William H. Jackson took his famous and widely-circulated photographs in the 1870s.

Hayden was shrewd enough to include Jackson in his 1873 exploration because the photographer's work not only brought worldwide attention to the Rocky Mountains, but also enhanced Hayden's position in requesting taxpayers' funds for future

ELBERT

This view of Mount Elbert — the state's highest peak, at an elevation of 14,433 feet — can be seen from just east of U.S. Highway 24, as you look toward the west.

ELBERT and MASSIVE

surveys. Jackson is generally credited with "discovering" Mount of the Holy Cross, but the mountain abounds in legend. According to one story, retold by author Perry Eberhart, two lost Spanish priests first saw the mountain in the 1700s. Barely alive, the priests became inspired when the clouds opened and revealed the cross. Taking new heart and new direction, the priests found their way back to what is now New Mexico.

The first recorded sighting of the Mount of the Holy Cross is believed to have been by William Brewer on August 29, 1869. He reportedly saw it from the summit of Grays Peak.

Jackson's first photograph of the Mount of the Holy Cross was taken on August 23, 1873. Reports that Jackson retouched the negatives, particularly the right arm of the cross, to make it straighter and brighter, have been disputed. Author William M. Bueler, now living in Winona, Minnesota, says that "Jackson retouched the cross not to make a more perfect cross than ever existed, but to make a cross that matched the more perfect cross that appears in his unretouched negatives of 1873. As Jackson commented in his book, *Time Exposure*, 'I have snapped my shutter morning, noon and afternoon [on his later visits]. And I have never come close to matching those first plates.' "

Ron Ruhoff of Evergreen, Colorado, in a letter to *Empire Magazine*, concurs:

> While Jackson certainly did retouch the cross on some of his negatives and even add a waterfall, he did not retouch the cross on all of them. In particular, the one and only 11-by-14 glass plate dated August 23, 1873, did not have a retouched cross, but nevertheless shows a perfect snow formation. I was fortunate enough to have inspected this plate and receive a print from it in 1958, prior to its breakage. Jackson made several photo trips to Notch Mountain in later years, but states in his writings that never was the cross as naturally perfect as his first expedition in 1873.

*S*outhwest of Leadville are Colorado's two highest mountains, less than three miles apart as the crow flies: Mount Elbert (left) and Mount Massive.

Ruhoff continues:

It is interesting to note that in Jackson's day the best snow conditions in the cross were found in the middle of August, while today one must view it around the first part of July, indicating much more snow in those days. There is also a new excellent viewpoint for the cross — heading west through the Eisenhower Tunnel on Interstate 70, one can see it plainly upon emerging from the West Portal.

Regardless of what Jackson saw and photographed in the 1870s, the cross is now less than perfect. Yet, it still is inspirational. The cross is 1,150 feet high, with arms 400 feet across; the crevices are 50 to 80 feet deep and 25 to 50 feet wide. The photographs of the Mount of the Holy Cross in this book were taken in early spring, when the peak was covered with snow. The outer fringes melt off in June and July, leaving snow only in the crevices, thus better outlining the cross.

Numerous pilgrimages have been made to the mountain, and many cures claimed by those who have prayed near it. A series of pilgrimages began after World War I — and preceded the popular journeys sponsored by *The Denver Post* starting in 1928.

As reported in a December 19, 1976, *Empire Magazine* story by Zeke Scher, *Denver Post* editor Frederick Gilmer Bonfils, on March 18, 1928,

MASSIVE

*B*oarded-up buildings on the outskirts of Leadville complement one view of Mount Massive, looking toward the west. In the bottom photo on the opposite page, Massive is seen from Colorado Highway 91 between Climax and Leadville. The photo above shows how 14,421-foot Massive looks from the air. Note the long ridge in the foreground.

MOUNT of the HOLY CROSS

announced the promotion of the "annual pilgrimage of Christians" each summer "from all over the world" to the Mount of the Holy Cross. With Al G. Birch, the *Post's* press agent for half a century, directing the project, the first pilgrimage in mid-July, 1928, attracted 188 persons from 25 states and Canada.

At that time, the shortest route to Minturn —

which is 11 miles from Notch Mountain's summit facing the cross — was 195 miles from Denver. It is now about 100 miles by way of Interstate 70. At Minturn, the pilgrims could walk the six miles to the base camp or rent a saddle horse for $2 per day.

In the spring of 1929, President Herbert Hoover signed a proclamation creating the Mount of the

*M*ount of the Holy Cross as seen 100 years apart. The 20th-Century air view at left was taken in early spring, while William Henry Jackson took his famous photo (below) in August, 1873.

William Henry Jackson original, now owned by Emma Lou (Daggett) Miles

76. MT OF THE HOLY CROSS.

In 1933, a shelter house was built on Notch Mountain facing Mount of the Holy Cross to provide pilgrims protection from storms. The shelter house is still in good condition and used by hikers today. Elevation of Mount of the Holy Cross is 14,005 feet.

Holy Cross National Monument, which set aside 1,392 acres within Holy Cross National Forest. In 1933, a shelter house was built of stone and timber on Notch Mountain to protect the pilgrims from storms, with windows looking out toward the cross. But then, interest began to wane, and the pilgrimages faded away in the mid-1930s following the death of F. G. Bonfils. The Holy Cross National Forest disappeared in 1945, being merged with the White River National Forest. In 1950, Congress abolished the Holy Cross National Monument, citing, among other reasons, a decline in interest in the monument.

Some 473,000 acres of the White River Forest are in the Holy Cross District, and Ernie Nunn, the district ranger at Minturn, reported that about 8,000 persons visited him during 1976, walking along good trails to the old shelter house. That summer, about 150 "pilgrims," led by Redcliff Mayor Manuel Martinez, journeyed to Notch Mountain to view the Mount of the Holy Cross and experience some of the inspiration that William H. Jackson no doubt felt when he focused his camera on the mountain a century earlier.

Jackson went on to more fame a year after he first photographed the mountain with the snowy cross. In 1874, he took pictures of the cliff dwellings and ancient Indian ruins in southwestern Colorado, and this was considered another "great discovery" by the Hayden Survey.

There was no doubt that Hayden and his men had popularized the wonders of the West.

MOUNT of the HOLY CROSS

Section Five . . .

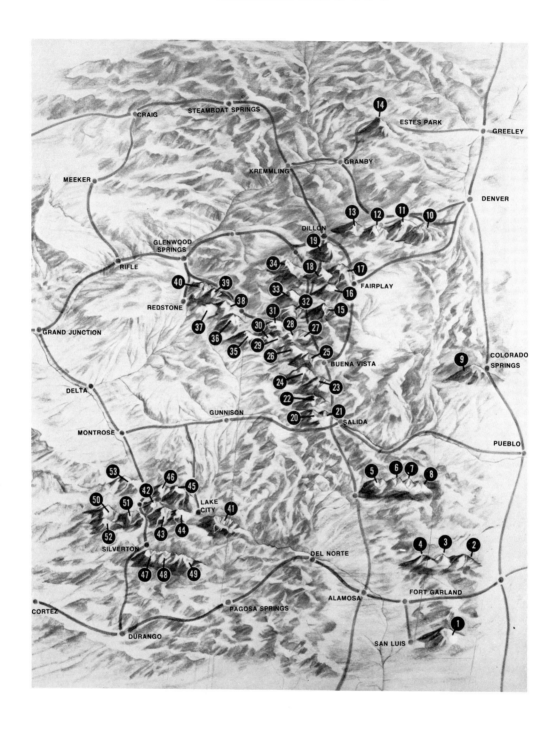

35	Castle Peak
36	Pyramid Peak
37	Maroon Peak
38	North Maroon Peak
39	Snowmass Peak
40	Capitol Peak

Elk Range

The Elk Mountain group is one of the most remarkable ranges in our Western territories and, so far as my own explorations have extended, is unique in form and structure.

F. V. Hayden, 1874

This mountain range, which stretches west of the Sawatch Range between the Roaring Fork and Gunnison River tributaries, offers some of the finest peaks in the Rockies — rugged and steep mountains in beautiful settings of tumbling streams, large lakes, grassy meadows, wildflowers, beaver ponds and aspen groves. That Hayden and his men were impressed is an understatement. Let's examine some of their writings.

Hayden, in his 1874 report, wrote:

The Elk Mountains reach out from near the headwaters of the Gunnison River, 40 miles to the northwest and, though generally not as high as the other ranges of northern Colorado, are by far the most rugged of them all . . . The gorges or canyons cut by Castle and Maroon creeks and their branches are probably without a parallel for ruggedness, depth and picturesque beauty in any portion of the West. The great variety of colors of the rocks, the remarkable and unique forms of the peaks, and the extreme ruggedness, all conspire to impress the beholder with wonder.

In that same report, William Henry Holmes, who made some remarkable panoramic sketches of Colorado's mountains, wrote:

. . . [we saw] our first view of the western faces of the Elk Mountains, and are impressed more deeply than ever with their beauty and grandeur . . .

The lower slopes are . . . densely covered by a growth of gray and purple underbrush. Above this, groves of aspens and clusters of dark blue pines relieve the glowing reds and purples of the carboniferous rocks. Still higher, and in delightful contrast to these ardent colors, are the summits of gray granite, whose polished and ornate faces constantly remind us of the form in some gothic cathedral.

After camping late one night near timberline, the Hayden men climbed up a high ridge the next morning and Holmes was inspired to write:

On the following two pages, the magnificence of the Elk Range is captured in an aerial photo looking toward the southeast. The prominent peak in the photo is Castle, encased in spring ice. Castle Peak is the 12th highest in Colorado.

CASTLE

We soon found ourselves in the midst of the mountains [with] Snowmass and Capitol to the east, [Mt.] Sopris alone at the north, and many groups of lofty mountains in the southwest. All around us were only bare rock and snow. The whole area is above timberline, and the sculpture of the mountains is wonderfully striking and picturesque.

And Henry Gannett, the famed topographer whose chief function was mapmaking, even took time to note that the Elk Mountain's "present great diversity of colors, some being of light gray trachyte, others of red, maroon and brown sandstone." He called Sopris, a pretty 12,823-foot peak north of Capitol Peak, "a very massive mountain."

The southernmost Fourteener in the Elks is Castle Peak, the highest in the range and No. 12 in Colorado with an elevation of 14,265 feet. It can be reached on the road due south of Aspen leading to Ashcroft. Castle, which was climbed and named by Hayden's men, was described this way by Gannett:

[It] has a conical summit, from which a main ridge runs south in a succession of high, needle-like points [which obviously impressed him as having the appearance of a castle]. The summit is well-nigh inaccessible, the only way to reach it being up a crevice on the south side . . . Its color is dark brown.

North of Castle is a peak named for Hayden. While Hayden and his men climbed many of Colorado's Highest for the first time, this peak carrying his name is 439 feet under 14,000.

Pyramid Peak, called a "first-class peak" by Gannett, is northwest of Castle Peak and southwest of Aspen, on the road to Maroon Lake. It also can be seen from about a mile southeast of Aspen on Colorado Highway 82. Ever since the Hayden and Wheeler surveys "discovered" its treacherous and perilous climbing conditions, Pyramid has remained one of the roughest mountains to ascend. These survey teams did not climb 14,018-foot Pyramid; one of Wheeler's men got to within 200 feet of the summit before being turned back by the mountain's steepness and loose sandstone.

A photographer's paradise best describes one of the state's most popular pair of mountains west of Pyramid Peak — Maroon Peak (also called South Maroon Peak) and North Maroon Peak. Rising majestically above Maroon Lake, the Maroon Bells — as they are popularly known — have claimed the lives of many climbers. Gannett of the Hayden Survey, in describing both of them as "Maroon Mountain," wrote:

[It] is so named from its peculiar color, that of the [dark-red] sandstones of which it is composed. It is one of the highest peaks in the system, and its summit [the elevation of Maroon Peak, second highest in the Elk

This aerial photo shows the proximity of Pyramid Peak (left) to the Maroon Bells.

Range, is 14,156 feet] is nearly, if not quite, inaccessible. On the north and south, it presents walls almost vertical for 2,000 feet; on the west it is full as steep for 3,000 feet, and on the east a sharp, comb-like ridge runs down from its summit . . .

Northwest of the Maroon Bells is Snowmass Mountain, which cannot be seen from any highway. Hayden said that the view "is very extended and grand" from the top of Snowmass and that the mountain was named for "an extensive snowfield" on its east face. If the unstable rock at its summit came tumbling down, the peak's elevation could be reduced by a couple hundred feet. But, until that

The photo on the opposite page shows the treacherous climbing conditions of Pyramid Peak. The photo of Pyramid above was taken from the road to Maroon Lake.

PYRAMID

MAROON BELLS

The Maroon Bells, southwest of Aspen, are a photographer's paradise. In a setting of rich blue sky and aspen trees at Maroon Lake are Maroon Peak and to the right, North Maroon Peak. Maroon Peak is 25th highest in Colorado, with an elevation of 14,156 feet; North Maroon ranks 49th at 14,014 feet.

day, Snowmass remains an impressive member of the Fourteeners Club with an elevation of 14,092 feet. It was one of the last mountains in Colorado to be calculated at 14,000 feet, and Hayden felt it was several feet below that mark. Experienced outdoorsmen refer to the snow on the peak as "watermelon snow," because the algae growing so prevalently there smells like watermelon.

Southeast of Snowmass is another photographer's dream — Hagerman Peak, which is 400 feet shy of being a Fourteener. It was named for Percy Hagerman, who climbed many of the mountains in the area and is believed to have been the first to make it to the top of Pyramid Peak.

Hagerman, along with Harold Clark, are said to have been the first to climb Capitol Peak, in 1909. Capitol, which is north of its "twin" peak, Snowmass, was named by the Hayden Survey. Some historians have credited Hayden, or his men, with being the first to ascend Capitol. Author William M. Bueler disputes this, pointing out that the Hayden Survey's reports make no mention of climbing it. Substantiating this claim are the 1874 writings of Hayden's topographer, Gannett:

(Capitol Peak is) one of the crowning summits of the range . . . whose gray, prism-shaped top and precipitous sides forbid access.

Capitol Peak also at one time was considered less than 14,000 feet high, but recent surveys make it Colorado's 30th highest at 14,130 feet.

It is interesting to reflect here that while the Hayden Survey missed on many calculations, the triangulated altitudes made by it are extremely close to those determined by much more thorough methods in later years. And, in his 1876 report, Hayden wasn't far off when he estimated that there were "about 50" mountains in Colorado over 14,000 feet.

It is fitting here, also, to repeat the tribute made to this Elk Range region by Jeremy Agnew of Colorado Springs in a June 1, 1975 story in *Empire Magazine*. Agnew, after visiting the Maroon Bells-Snowmass wilderness area about 10 miles southwest of Aspen and containing 66,000 acres of natural beauty from the valley of the Roaring Fork to the snow-capped Fourteeners, made a plea for all men and women to conserve the wilderness. He wrote of . . .

. . . cool, dark pine forests, rushing mountain streams and grassy meadows, covered in June and July with wildflower carpets of reds, yellows, blues and purples. Deer, elk, bobcats and beavers live in these mountains, along with squirrels, chipmunks, marmots . . . Little streams rush down from melting snowbanks to water

MAROON BELLS

*M*ountain climbers long have found the Maroon Bells a stiff challenge. Many inexperienced climbers, however, have underestimated the difficulties in ascending the peaks, and have paid for it with their lives.

105

MAROON BELLS

This seldom seen view — from the air — shows the backside of the Maroons.

the lush subalpine meadows, strewn with the blooms of columbine, bistort and Parry's primrose. I saw a fat marmot sunning on a rock and heard a pika squeaking and whistling as he scurried around gathering sedges and grasses to store for his winter food supply. I watched a hawk circle in the blue sky, riding the air currents and looking for an unsuspecting victim for lunch. This was the mountain wilderness experience we had come to enjoy . . .

The days of the frontier woodsman are gone and the day of the educated backpacker is here. The West has been won, but without the care of many people, this beautiful wilderness could easily be lost.

In the photo on the opposite page, algae — an early spring condition — forms streaks in the snow atop Snowmass Peak. Another aerial view above (the peak cannot be seen from any highway) shows the snowfield on Snowmass' east face, from which the mountain got its name.

SNOWMASS

The aerial photo on the opposite page shows the Capitol Peak area, while the photo above, looking south up Capitol Creek, provides a good view of the summit. Capitol Peak is known for its thin ridges and knife edge.

CAPITOL

Section Six . . .

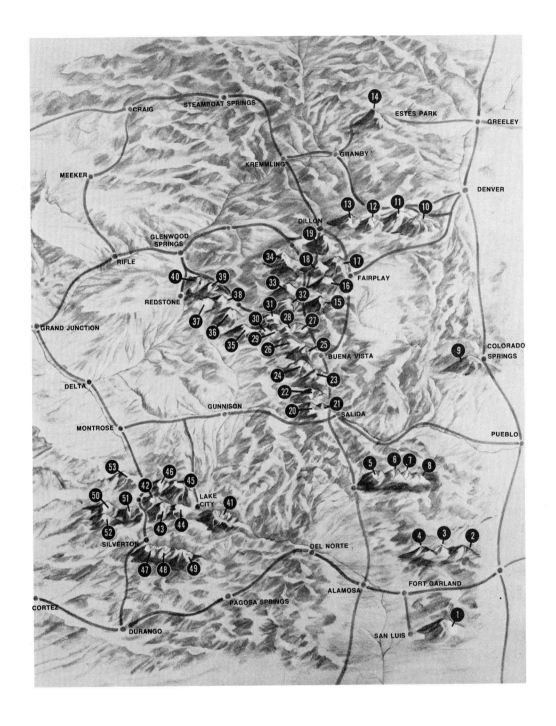

41	San Luis Peak	**45**	Uncompahgre Peak	**50**	Wilson Peak
42	Handies Peak	**46**	Wetterhorn Peak	**51**	Mount Wilson
43	Redcloud Peak	**47**	Mount Eolus	**52**	El Diente Peak
44	Sunshine Peak	**48**	Sunlight Peak	**53**	Mount Sneffels
		49	Windom Peak		

San Juan and San Miguel Ranges

In some places the numbers of the pinnacles massed behind one another presented the appearance of church spires, only built after a much grander style of architecture than most of our modern religious edifices.

Franklin Rhoda, Hayden Survey, 1874

The Fourteeners in the San Juan Mountains, which Henry Gannett of the Hayden Survey called "an immense, rugged nucleus from which radiate in all directions heavy, long spurs," include the three Needle Mountains above Durango in the Weminuche Wilderness, groupings northwardly in the Lake City-Ouray area, the isolated San Luis Peak to the east and, to the west, three peaks in the San Miguel Range, which is a westward extension of the San Juan uplift.

In other words: Whew! This is a massive mountain area making up a great portion of the southwest quarter of Colorado. Besides Gannett and Rhoda, other Hayden men were equally impressed. A. D. Wilson said the San Juans were "a peculiarly massive range, composed almost entirely of volcanic rocks." Frederic M. Endlich, the survey's scientist, wrote:

> Numerous points of great beauty in detail, colors in great variety, exhibiting many shades . . . greatly add to the effect produced by the almost ideal shape of peaks and ridges. [There are] formations of thousands of little pinnacles, not unlike Gothic architecture in appearance . . . Rugged and steep is the character of the mountain sides.

Endlich was one of Hayden's men who made special note in their reports of experiencing a fantastic phenomenon while exploring Colorado's higher mountains: "Large quantities of electricity." When there was electricity in the atmosphere, he wrote, "any metal instrument . . . would produce a buzzing sound like the hammer of an induction-coil . . . Electricity grew so large and intense that I received from my rifle a shock

On the following pages, Stewart Peak is visible on the left-hand page; it once was considered a Fourteener. Far to the right looms San Luis Peak with an elevation of 14,014 feet.

SAN LUIS

This aerial view of Handies Peak shows the graceful slopes of the mountain, which is the 40th highest in Colorado.

sufficient to paralyze me momentarily." Later, Endlich continued, "every hair on my head was rising upward . . . every finger buzzed when held up into the air, and every pointed rock hummed with a sonorous sound."

But it was the sensations experienced by A. D. Wilson and Franklin Rhoda while atop Uncompahgre Peak and, in particular, Sunshine Peak in the San Juans that were most spectacular. And these same electrical sensations have been experienced since then by many climbers venturing into the Colorado Rockies. More about this later.

The easternmost peak of the San Juans, 14,014-foot San Luis, was named for the valley below it. The peak is almost due north of Creede and is one that cannot be seen from the road. San Luis is on a smooth ridge with three other peaks to the north, including 13,983-foot Stewart Peak that once was considered a Fourteener.

Northwest of Lake City are two Fourteeners, Uncompahgre and Wetterhorn peaks, that can be

HANDIES

This photo of Handies taken in the summer shows the peak's relatively easy hiking conditions.

REDCLOUD

Redcloud Peak is aptly named, as evidenced by the photo on the opposite page. The peak once was called Red Mountain.

seen from Slumgullion Pass on Colorado Highway 149 at Windy Point. Uncompahgre at one time was considered to be the highest mountain in Colorado, but it now is officially No. 6, with an elevation of 14,309 feet. The peak is named after the Uncompahgre River, which is a corruption of a Ute Indian word meaning either "red lake" or "hot spring."

Rhoda, who — as we have mentioned — climbed Uncompahgre Peak with Wilson during a violent thunderstorm in the summer of 1874, said the mountain's "striking resemblance to the profile of the Matterhorn gave us a wholesome dread of it, for as yet it had never been ascended by anyone, and we felt that to reach the summit might be beyond the range of the possible." Starting out early one morning and "expecting a very difficult climb," the men "found the ascent very easy and arrived on the summit at 7:30 a.m., having been 2½ hours climbing up 2,400 feet." They found the summit "quite smooth" and, as Rhoda noted, "to the south the peaks appeared in great numbers, and in the distance appeared a group of very scraggy mountains, about which clouds were circling, as if it was their home." Earlier in the climb, the men "were terribly taken aback when, at elevation of over 13,000 feet, a she-grizzly with her two cubs came rushing past us from the top of the peak."

Wetterhorn Peak is three miles west of Uncompahgre, separated by another impressive mountain (though not a Fourteener), Matterhorn Peak (elevation 13,590 feet). The Wheeler Survey reportedly named Wetterhorn for the famed Swiss mountain.

Southwest of Lake City are three Fourteeners — Sunshine, Redcloud and Handies, all neighbors bringing up the rear of Colorado's Highest. In fact, some dispute Sunshine Peak's membership in the club of 53 peaks rising 14,000 feet or higher. Still, its official elevation is 14,001, ranking it last among the state's Fourteeners. Redcloud Peak's elevation also is suspect, but remains at 14,034 feet for 45th place. One of Colorado's least-seen mountains, it probably was named for its redness and sweeping ridges that resemble clouds. Handies Peak is 40th highest, with an elevation of 14,048 feet; it is west of Sunshine and Redcloud. Sunshine, once known as Sherman Mountain, can be seen from Windy Point on Slumgullion Pass and from the road above Lake San Cristobal. Redcloud, north of Sunshine, can be seen best from the west looking east, on a four-wheel-drive road. Handies, reportedly named after a prominent pioneer of the area, also can be reached via four-wheeler, after passing Redcloud Peak.

The aerial photo above, taken from the southeast, shows Sunshine Peak on the left and Redcloud to the right. The photo of Sunshine on the opposite page was taken from the road that passes by San Cristobal Lake.

SUNSHINE and REDCLOUD

While Sunshine Peak is the lowest of all the Fourteeners in Colorado, it received considerable mention in Hayden's 1874 report because of the electrical storm Rhoda and Wilson experienced on its summit. Rhoda referred to the peak merely as "Station 12" and estimated its height as 13,967 feet. Here is his account of that memorable day:

Rhoda and Wilson were working on the mountain when they felt a "peculiar tickling sensation along the roots of the hair" caused by electricity in the air. "By holding up our hands above our heads, a tickling sound was produced, which was still louder if we held a hammer or other instrument in our hand." This sensation, he continued, was accompanied by "a peculiar sound almost exactly like that produced by frying bacon . . . This phenomenon, when continued for any length of time, becomes highly monotonous and disagreeable."

Rhoda explained that as the electricity increased "the instrument on the tripod began to click like a telegraph machine when it is made to work

From Windy Point on Slumgullion Pass, this panoramic view shows two of the more photogenic Fourteeners: Wetterhorn Peak, to the left, and Uncompahgre Peak, to the right. In the photo at the left is Uncompahgre, looking east; in the photo at right, you are looking west-southwest toward Uncompahgre, with Wetterhorn in the background.

WETTERHORN and UNCOMPAHGRE

rapidly." He also noticed that "the pencils in our fingers made a similar, but finer sound whenever we let them lie back so as to touch the flesh of the hand between the thumb and forefinger." He said the sound "at first is a continuous series of clicks . . . but the intervals became less and less, till finally a musical sound results."

There were a few minutes of relief, Rhoda explained, but following a clap of thunder, lightning struck a nearby peak, discharging more electricity. The tickling and "hair-frying" started all over again, this time in quicker succession and with louder sounds. After noting that the "clouds settled into the Great Canyon of the Lake Fork and boiled about in a curious manner," Rhoda displayed his sense of humor when he wrote:

By this time [our] work was getting exciting. We were electrified, and our notes were taken and recorded with lightning speed, in keeping with the terrible tension of the storm cloud's electricity.

When they raised their hats, "our hair stood on end." And, while the sharp points of the stones emitted a continuous sound, "the instrument outsang everything else."

As the lightning strokes came thicker and faster, and their barometer hummed louder and louder,

In the photo on the preceding page, the magnitude of Wetterhorn Peak is apparent when compared to the size of the trees in the foreground. The photo above is an opposite view of Wetterhorn, looking east.

WETTERHORN

125

*A*t left is a view of Mount Eolus from Columbine
Pass. The mountain's round summit also is visible
in the photo taken from the air (above).

EOLUS

*H*ere are three views of Sunlight Peak: The east side (above) from Vallecito Creek; an aerial view (below) showing the southwest face, and the west side of the mountain (opposite page) from Columbine Pass.

Rhoda and Wilson figured it was time to leave the summit. Both men were stubborn about leaving, since they didn't want to climb the mountain again the next day to finish their surveying, mapping and sketching.

They crawled down the side of the peak, lying low between some rocks. "The points of the angular stones being of different degrees of sharpness," Rhoda wrote, "each produced a sound peculiar to itself." Nothing like being serenaded while waiting out an electrical storm.

Wilson, who had left his instrument on the summit when he dashed for cover, went back up

SUNLIGHT

A neighbor of Sunlight Peak, Windom Peak (above) also can be seen from Vallecito Creek. The photo on the opposite page provides us with a different view of Windom.

WINDOM

for it on his hands and knees, "seized the tripod and flung it over his shoulder, [receiving] a strong electrical shock as if the sharp-point instrument had pierced his shoulder." Wilson dropped the brass cap that protected the "object-glass" of the telescope, but he didn't go back for it. Rhoda and Wilson quickly went down the southeast side of the peak; when they were about 30 feet from the summit, lightning struck where they had been stationed. "We had only just missed it," Rhoda said, "and felt thankful for our narrow escape." They then were drenched by hail and rain.

Commenting later on this and similar experiences, especially in the San Juans, Rhoda said:

> The romance connected with these phenomena had all disappeared — thereafter whenever our hair began to fry, we generally disappeared at pretty short notice.

South of both Sunshine Peak and Silverton are the Needle Mountains: Eolus, Sunlight and

Windom. One prevailing feature of this area is the wind, and 14,084-foot Mount Eolus was no doubt named for the Greek god of winds, Aeolus, soon after the Hayden Survey visited the region in 1874. Eolus, due north of Bayfield and U.S. Highway 160, can be reached either from Vallecito Creek and over Columbine Pass, or from the D&RGW rail head at Needleton, then up Chicago Basin deep in the Weminuche Wilderness.

Sunlight Peak (14,059 feet) which is flanked by Eolus and Windom, can be seen from Columbine Pass, but better viewed from Vallecito Creek north of the Vallecito Reservoir. It reportedly was named in 1902 by the Geological Survey.

Windom Peak (14,087 feet), on the same ridge as Sunlight and southeast of it, can be seen from

How a bird would see them (above): Wilson Peak in foreground, Mount Wilson in far left background and El Diente in right background. On opposite page is an autumn shot of Wilson Peak.

MOUNT WILSON, WILSON PEAK, EL DIENTE

133

The blue mountain is El Diente, as seen from the meadows. The mountain features a ragged outline and is 24th highest in Colorado.

134

THE HAYDEN SURVEY CREW, camped on the flatlands near the mountains.

Vallecito Creek looking west. It apparently is a coincidence that windswept Windom Peak is so named; records show it was named for a politician at the turn of the century, William Windom, who once served Uncle Sam as secretary of the treasury.

Northwest of the Needle Mountains are the three Fourteeners in the San Miguel Range: Wilson Peak, Mount Wilson and El Diente Peak, which William H. Holmes of the Hayden Survey called "one of the finest groups of summits in the Rocky Mountains, and viewed from the north (they) present a magnificent panorama." Franklin Rhoda felt Mount Wilson was "the highest mountain in southwestern Colorado, and by far the most massive." Actually, Mount Wilson (14,246 feet) is the second highest in the San Juan and San Miguel ranges (Uncompahgre is higher at 14,309 feet), and the 16th highest in Colorado.

Both of the Wilsons were *not* named for the 28th President of the United States, but for A. D. Wilson of the Hayden Survey. It is interesting to note that Rhoda, in his report, pointed out that while they were climbing Mount Wilson, "Mr. Wilson succeeded in killing a fair-sized male grizzly with his Springfield needle-gun."

EL DIENTE

EL DIENTE

Wilson Peak (14,017 feet) can be seen from Colorado Highway 145 southwest of Telluride. Mount Wilson, about 1½ miles as the crow flies south of Wilson Peak, cannot be seen from the highway. Jagged and steep El Diente Peak (14,159 feet), whose name in Spanish means "tooth," is to the west of Mount Wilson and on the same ridge. It can be seen from the Dunton road, west of Colorado Highway 145.

East of Mount Wilson is the unusual Lizard Head, a volcanic neck whose elevation is 13,113 feet. Frederic M. Endlich of the Hayden Survey called it "a curious monument of trachyte, an obelisk-like mass of stone placed upon a natural pedestal, of symmetrical form." Author Robert Ormes says Lizard Head is "the most difficult of Colorado's summits to reach" and that the "rottenness of its 400-foot rock tower makes safety too much a matter of luck for comfort."

North and east of these mountains, west of Ouray and southwest of Ridgway, is one of Colorado's most beautiful (and most photographed) peaks — 14,150-foot Mount Sneffels. It can be seen from Colorado Highway 62 over Dallas Divide. The Mount Sneffels Mining District, which included great wealth-producing mines within a few miles of the famous mountain on the sides of other mountains and canyons nearby, probably was the richest area in the nation.

Rhoda felt "both deep respect and awe" for Sneffels. Climbing it with Rhoda were Wilson, Endlich and a packer. In a letter to *Empire Magazine*, Mel Griffiths of Denver gave some interesting details about the climb and how Sneffels got its name:

> The ascent was made on September 10, 1874. The approach was from the headwaters of Deep Creek, on the Telluride side of the range. They climbed in one day over the saddle at the head of Deep Creek, down into Blue Lakes Basin at the head of Dallas Creek on the north side of the range, then to Blue Lakes Pass and up the southwest ridge of the peak.
>
> They spent two hours on the summit making observations and returned to their camp on Deep Creek about 8 p.m., having walked about six miles of horizontal distance and 7,000 vertical feet each way. In his account, Rhoda calls the mountain Sneffels without referring to how it got the name. In William M. Bueler's book, *Roof of the Rockies*, an explanation is given.

Far in the background — looking west from an airplane — El Diente, Mount Wilson and Wilson Peak rise above very rugged terrain. Just to the left of El Diente is a well-known landmark, Lizard Head.

and the WILSONS

137

SNEFFELS

Some years after the climb, Dr. Endlich told the story to Frederick Chapin, who published it in 1890 in *Appalachia*, a mountaineering journal.

Dr. Endlich's recollection was that while crossing Blue Lakes Basin, one member of the party likened it to the great hole in the earth described by Jules Verne in *A Journey to the Center of the Earth*. Dr. Endlich agreed and, pointing to the great brooding peak hovering over the basin, said: "There's Snaefell," referring to the Icelandic mountain which Verne describes near the hole.

By that time, perhaps for novelistic purposes, Verne had modified the name of the Icelandic mountain to Sneffels, which became the name given the Colorado peak by the Hayden Survey.

The aerial view above of Mount Sneffels looks northwest toward Uncompahgre Plateau. The view of Sneffels on the opposite page looks to the south, also from the air.

SNEFFELS

This is how Mount Sneffels appears in the summer. The photo was taken from a point east of U.S. Highway 550 between Ridgway and Ouray.

140

FRESH AIR and exercise in the mountains made the simple meals taste better for the Hayden Survey team.

SNEFFELS

Golden aspens complement the autumn scene of beautiful Mount Sneffels, one of the most-photographed mountains in Colorado. Views similar to this one on the opposite page can be seen from Colorado Highway 62 over Dallas Divide.

That night, back at camp after climbing Mount Sneffels, Rhoda reported cheerily that the men "had the pleasure of sitting down to a supper which tasted far better than the most costly meals of civilization, served up in the most expensive hotels."

A simple meal, no doubt, but made tastier by the excitement and satisfaction of their accomplishments that day.

On another occasion, Rhoda wrote:

> We find sufficient time while climbing to observe the scenery around us in a very general way, but the romance of our work is not fully appreciated by us till we reach civilization where we can find leisure to think over what we have seen.

As long as there are mountains, there will be romance in climbing their challenging cliffs . . . or in merely looking at their snow-capped peaks from afar . . . or in just knowing that they belong to you and me. That is the comfort of *Colorado's Highest.*

END

GEORGE CROUTER

It takes an avid outdoorsman like George Crouter, with a special talent for taking photographs, to record for us his appreciation for Nature. His favorite sport is sailing (he owns two sailboats and you can find him and his family on an area lake just about any warm weekend). But Crouter is at home also on a horse trekking deep into wilderness country or in an airplane flying over his beloved Rocky Mountains, taking pictures for *Empire Magazine,* a Sunday publication of *The Denver Post.* Crouter has been with the *Post* for 15 years, including 12 years on the *Empire* staff. Before joining the *Post* as a news photographer, Crouter was on a similar assignment for 7 years at the *Pueblo* (Colorado) *Star Journal and Chieftain.*

Crouter was born in Wheatland, Wyoming; he attended Colorado State University in Fort Collins when it was known as Colorado A&M, and later received a bachelor of science degree from the University of Denver. During his college days, he was active in gymnastics and was a member of the pistol team.

Crouter's photographs have not gone unrecognized, and his citations include one from *Editor and Publisher Magazine* for an *Empire* cover, judged best in the U.S. for creative use of editorial photography.

Crouter and his wife, who have two daughters, live in southeast Denver. During World War II he served 3 years in the Merchant Marine and later was in the Army Reserve.